Wittgenstein's Football Tactics
& Other Poems

This is the second poetry collection by former teacher, **Tim Hopkins**, the first having been entitled, *Epitaph for an Auctioneer & Other Poems.* In addition to poetry for adults and children, Tim Hopkins has published two novels for teenagers, and written humorous material for comedians and cartoonists. He has also composed songs that have been performed and recorded in the UK and the USA.

By the same Author -

Epitaph for an Auctioneer
& Other Epigrams

On Target
a football novel aimed at young teens

Jimmy Swift
a football novel aimed at mid-teens and older

Nobody Pushes Me Around
an illustrated football story for 'improving'
readers of secondary school age

Wittgenstein's
Football Tactics
& Other Poems

Tim Hopkins

Arena Books

First published in 2020 by Arena Books

Arena Books
6 Southgate Green
Bury St. Edmunds
IP33 2BL

www.arenabooks.co.uk

*Distributed in America by Ingram International, One Ingram
Blvd., P.O. Box 3006, La Vergne, TN 37086-1985, USA.*

Tim Hopkins
Wittgenstein's Football Tactics & *Other Poems*

British Library cataloguing in Publication Data. A Catalogue
record for this book is available from the British Library.

ISBN-13   978-1-911593-81-2
BIC classifications:- DCF.

Cover design
by Anna Gatt

Typeset in
Times New Roman

CONTENTS

1
The Moments in Between

The lemon light of daybreak is the sunset glowing red,
The seed-corn in the furrow has the scent of baking bread,
The acorn freshly planted forms a canopy of green
When we take away the moments in between.

The houses we're constructing have their demolition planned,
The ocean's rocky shoreline is a level beach of sand,
The unworked clay is Wedgwood, uncut stone, a figurine,
When we take away the moments in between.

Dr Johnson dines with Plato, Buddha counsels Henry Ford,
David's slingstone fells Carnera, Custer routs the Mongol horde,
Isaac Stern duets with Nero, Dante pines for Norma Jean,
When we take away the moments in between.

The hour of our birth is the hour of our death,
The first bewildered cry is the last defiant breath,
Eternity's the instant where the infinite is seen
When we take away the moments in between.

2
In the Planetarium

The commentary spoke of unimaginable distances,
Black holes and quasars,
The humble stellar geography of our doomed planet:
The while my tongue sought out an ulcer
Freshly launched on an inside cheek;
Had I bitten it at breakfast?
Would it heal of itself?
As I pondered these questions
A sepulchral voice worked its counterpoint,
Consigning our world to its modest place
In the expanding vastness,
Perhaps a cream would help?

3
Poetic Justice

My father makes Kafka's look kindly,
Balzac Mère next to mine is a saint,
Young Romulus shames my twin brother,
My sister makes Borden look quaint.

Disaffection converts into poems –
Despairing, yet lovingly wrought –
But when I commend them to *Faber*,
They're spiked with a sniffy retort.

To deaden the pain of rejection
I bungee jump tied at the chin,
Play Russian Roulette with five bullets,
Scratch oaths in my flesh with a pin.

Self-torture results in new poems,
Eclipsing original hurt,
I pop into *Cape* with the typescript,
Who dish me the long-winded dirt.

At this I renounce my creations,
In truth, Mum and Dad are great fun,
My brother and sister quite charming,
And bogus malaise overdone.

4
Squeezed

Time's Accordion
Extends for the music of childhood
Contracts for the silence of age.

5
Living Hell

Hell's ourselves, not other people,
And Sartre got it wrong,
The human tones we most revile
But echo our own song,
For hell is being out of key
With cosmic concert pitch
(The conscience, like a tuning fork,
Betrays discordant kitsch)
Such private inharmonic pain
In vain we disavow:
When hell is dissonance within,
We face the music now.

6
Paradoxical

The Oppressor brutalises himself
But those he subdues have their dignity;
The slanderer sinks barbs in his own flesh
But those he vilifies are free of hurt;
The liar's distortion blurs his vision
But those he deceives improve their focus;
The thief deprives himself of his value
But his victim's loss is replaceable;
Faithless lovers become lonely strangers
But those they betray are silent allies.

7
Relatively Speaking

The latest academic fad
Asserts that nothing's good or bad,
It's *relative* we're archly told,
(But so, of course, are hot and cold)
King Lear or Noddy? How to judge?
Is caviar compared with fudge?
Or Patience Strong with David Hume?
(Distinctions moulder in the tomb)
Now vintage claret, now Sauterne,
Who dares a variance discern?
Now rugby songs, now Turandot,
Disparity you mustn't spot,
Now Andy Warhol, now Cézanne,
No contrast mars the modish scan,
No strong, no weak, no rich, no poor,
Informed opinion is no more,
And Leonardo, Mozart, Blake,
Have had their day for pity's sake,
No gold, no dross, no gem, no jade,
Now everybody makes the grade
And each has fifteen minutes' fame –
Gossamer in Wisdom's flame.

8
The Second Coming

To Christians, Christ's return to earth,
Their faith is based upon,
But perhaps in this venal world of ours
Unnoticed he's been and gone.

9
Who

Who despairs of content may be content with despair,
Who lives in hope must hope to live,
Who is friend to all is not all friend,
Who boasts of honour may not honour the boast,
Who assumes he is correct cannot correct what he assumes.

10
Every Cloud…

Office bomb scare, twenty fifteen,
Left my psyche in a mess,
Fifteen grand in compensation
Eased my post-traumatic stress.

Stuffy workplace, twenty sixteen,
Spluttered, coughed and choked a lot,
Ailing colleagues caused the tickle,
Twenty K soon swelled the pot.

Missed promotion, twenty seventeen,
Overlooked on gender grounds,
Sex discrimination proven,
Netting thirty thousand pounds.

Fingers seized up twenty eighteen,
New equipment did the deed,
RSI, the diagnosis,
Forty 'thou' the sum agreed.

Acapulco, twenty nineteen,
Exemplar of perfect health,
Cured by specialists – my lawyers –
With the wonder drug of wealth.

11
Never

Never borrow from lenders keen to lend,
Never underinvest or overspend,
Never ride to fall or fear to ascend,
Never ingratiate or condescend.

Never ask cynics to help or defend,
Never trust those whose wit is to offend,
Never meet the friends your friends recommend,
Never cling to the past or embrace a trend.

12
Ruminants

Of critical texts
There's a palpable flood –
Scholars chewing
Another's cud.

13
SHAKESPEARE

SEEK A PHRASE

SEE A SPARK, EH?

AH, SPEAK SEER!

HE'S ERA'S PEAK.

14
Concurrent

Verbal felicity
Creates electricity
But critics' reviews
May blow the fuse.

15
Inglorious

From literary hearses
His mortal verses
Were taken unread
And interred – enough said.

16
Astronomical

The stars we praise
Shone years ago
For poets all
A massive blow.

17
Contentious

Messrs Anti and Pro
Exhaled much hot air,
But there's no word from either
In the graveyard they share.

18
References

The asterisk leads the eye of the sage
To recondite notes at the foot of the page,
While asterisk clusters in less worthy tomes
Conceal the locations where a lusty hand roams.

19
Philosophical

"*Cogito ergo sum,*" said René.
"I think therefore I am,"
Words echoed when drowning by Benét –
"I sink therefore I swam."

20
The Art of Football

Liverpool and Everton drew
Arsenal and Tottenham coloured in.

21
Advice to Footballers Who Have to Make a Speech

Kick off on time,
Cover the ground,
Make your position clear,
Throw in the odd joke,
Drive home your message,
Avoid extra time.

22
A Footballer from the Past

The dubbined boots with rounded caps
That took an age to lace,
The bulky shin-pads, baggy shorts,
The dour and weathered face;
A modest man whose sporting roots
Were deep in local soil,
Whose skills in bud and blossom
Would thrive and never spoil;
No vain and foolish self-regard,
No shameless mock distress,
No petulance, no schooled dissent,
No tantrums in the Press:
Instead a sense of privilege,
A pleasure in the game,
A dignity and self-respect
Unspoilt by easy fame.

23
FOOTBALL NEWS

ORIENT BEEF NO MATCH FOR WEST HAM

MOTHERWELL AS EXPECTED AFTER CLINICAL HEARTS JOB

NO ROOM FOR CHESTERFIELD AT TIGHT VILLA

FOREST PLUNDERED BY WOLVES

NO RANGERS PICNIC AT QUEEN'S PARK

UPPITY YORK TAMED BY PALACE

CITY POUNDED BY GUNNERS

HULL STUCK IN MUD AT PORTSMOUTH

24
Wittgenstein's Football Tactics

The World Cup is all that is in the case.
Each country can be in the Cup or not in the Cup.
A fixture represents a possible situation in logical space.
While everything else remains the same, in tactics nothing is accidental.
If I can imagine players combined, I cannot imagine them excluded from the *possibility* of such combinations.
I call the sign with which we express a thought a propositional sign.
A ball in the spatial field though it need not be white must have some colour.
The ball whereof we cannot speak we must pass over in silence.

25
Love Story

He trails . . . . . She avails,
He sidles . . . . She idles,
He smiles . . . . She wiles,
He charms . . . .She disarms,
He pledges . . . She hedges,
He dares . . . . . She ensnares.

26
Enigma

We say the least
To those we desire
A tongue-tied coldness
Borne of fire.

27
Misalliance

Your safely centred values
My subversions underpin,
You're the tangent to my circle
From the outside looking in.

A web of surface parallels
Alluringly we spin,
But a hair's breadth is a light year
From the outside looking in.

28
Taking the Temperature

You love too little,
I love too much,
You're ice, I'm fire,
And when we touch,
I hope my warmth
Will make you stay,
But being ice
You melt away.

29
Winning Ways

My solicitor's good at divorces,
Tempers justice with cultural forces,
He shows a not uncompassionate touch,
Neither settles too small, nor asks too much,
With nebulous hurts enshrined as causes,
Children squeezed into hand-me-down clauses,
Silent T's crossed and tearful I's dotted,
The spoils of failure are soon allotted:
Emotion expressed in terms of the law,
And what's left of love locked up in a drawer.

30
Rapprochement

A woman without a man is like a fish without a bicycle.
(Gloria Steinem)

I point to a truth – I've no dirt to dish –
They've much in common, bicycles and fish:
In shops they're often suspended from hooks,
They're enemies of worms, on roads, in brooks;
Both need oil for maximum enjoyment,
Each provides leisure and employment,
Special equipment injects each with air,
At night they reflect a car headlights' glare;
Movement for each is restricted by locks,
Production's increased for depleted stocks;
They're so much alike the fish and the bike –
Perhaps Melissa has need of her Mike?

31
The Food of Love

Lettuce see
How mangoes about it...

First a plaice
Where singles meat:
You pear off
Let love flour
Offer your sole
Keep herbicide you
Never in salt

Pepper up the passion
Amaize her...

Undercurrants?
Don't believe everything you're herring
But know when your thyme is up:
Accept it with a rye smile
Eggs it gracefully.

32
The Fury

Scissors have sliced up his dress-suit,
The bath brims with claret and scotch,
His Mahler CDs have been bludgeoned,
A hammer applied to his watch.

His credit card's been through the shredder,
A scalpel has silenced his harp,
A solvent corrodes his Mercedes,
His Hockney discomfits his carp.

His golf clubs protrude from the cesspit,
His Wedgwood tureen's been dispatched,
His prize-winning marrow's been stamped on,
His Sheraton table is scratched.

You ask if his marriage is happy
In view of this virulent strife:
It is – the avenger's a lover –
Incensed he's gone back to his wife.

33
The Inventory

The *Martin Amis* with the wine stain on,
The Mozart CD with *Cosi* and *The Don*,
The Truffaut DVD you bought me in France,
The boxed set (scratched) of Gregorian chants,
The *Seamus Heaney* with the page ripped out,
The earthenware pot with the broken spout:
Leave them in a bag – I'll collect first thing –
Keep, if you like, the eternity ring.

34
A Snowflake Epithalamium

Let's toast the couple, Jack and Joy,
While there's some sparkle still,
For passion, like spumante,
Can be a short-lived thrill.

And Jack may yet be Joyless,
If Joy her bags should pack,
And Jack could tire of surfeit Joy,
And Joy be on her jack.

But should our bride and bridegroom
Through tacky times stick fast,
The bond may test credulity –
Like Superglue – and last.

35
Looking Forward

Saturdays we go to town
On disturbing buses
With exits so narrow
Two can never pass equally:
This is a portent –
One of us dies last.

36
Conundrums

It has a heart that cannot beat,
The lettuce in our salad treat.

It has a tongue but cannot speak,
The shoe that barely makes a squeak.

It moves in vessels that have no crew,
This trick the human blood can do.

You see its scales but hear no tune,
The leaping fish beneath the moon.

It has three hips but never thighs,
The loud hooray the cheerer cries.

Ears it has but hears no sounds,
The wheat that in the fields abounds.

It has an eye but cannot see,
The fierce tornado spinning free.

37
Lowland Dawn

A tidal wave of light
Bursts the horizon's bank
Flooding the black canvas of night
With the amber wash of morning.

38
Undercurrents

Ebbing waves
Approach with a whisper
Retreat with a chuckle.

39
Snowy Woods Revisited

Whose woods these are I think I know,
His HQ's in the city though,
Securicameras film us here
Our trespasses in court to show.

My little son, says, "Dad, it's queer
The owner never visits here."
I chide, "Don't come the William Blake,
The shares are up – we shouldn't sneer."

He gives his doubting head a shake:
"But surely, Dad, there's some mistake
When we can't stop and take a peep
At snow-lined trees and frozen lake."

They're selling high and buying cheap
Who from the poor this beauty keep:
The devil laughs, the angels weep,
The devil laughs, the angels weep.

(After Robert Frost)

40
Serendipity

I like to travel the unmarked ways
Where rooming houses offer no apologies
Where backstreet cafes are loud with dialect
And passers-by have private purposes,
Where the streets are warm with bread and kitchens
Where unrehearsed churches nestle in corners
And sudden squares surprise with their beauty.

41
Return to the Town of my Childhood

My hand rubbing the misted windscreen
Must have looked faintly regal
To the flag-waving crowds
Who had not turned out to greet me.

42
The Shadow

As the sun to the moon
So a parent to a favoured child
Bestowing a concentrated bounty:
But such a child – like the moon –
Has a cold and dark side.

43
Succession

When parents die
Inheritance flowers:
We don't step into their shoes –
They step into ours.

44
Within

Once upon a time there was time itself,
And in that time there was space,
And in that space was a world,
And in that world was a person,
And in that person was a brain,
And in that brain was a thought,
And in that thought, this poem.

45
French Leave

A shop-boy in sunny Marseilles
From Madame received little in peilles,
One morning quite weary
Phoned in and said, "Dearie,
I'm having a lie-in todeilles."

46
Retailer

A friendly butcher
The attentive type,
Sold and heard
A deal of tripe.

47
Beautiful Big

Beware the lean and hungry look
Which Caesar rightly feared,
The skinny man to stratagem
And spitefulness is geared.
Would Cassius at fourteen stone
Have felt the need to bitch?
And would Iago, fuller-faced
Have queered Othello's pitch?
It's well-observed how cheerfulness
Is found in well-filled suits,
As those who value sweetness know
To seek out softer fruits.
So let us laud the larger man
Devoid of schemes and wiles,
Whose munching muscles swell the cheeks
And wreathe a face in smiles.

48
Communication

Words we speak
The false, the true,
Are sound waves
Borne on CO_2 .

49
Popular Publishing

You turn away new talent
As first books rarely pay,
While signing up non-writers
With nothing much to say:
That overrated film star
Whose sex life counts as news,
That loutish chat-show junkie
Who can't resist the booze,
That puffed-up mediocrity
Whose name inspires a groan,
The 'sex and shopping' harpy
Who's known for being known...

Let 'friendly' TV programmes
Set up the PR con,
Where criticism's muted
And every goose a swan;
Your list soon floods the market
Restricting reader choice,
Meanwhile the sale of film rights
Provides your first Rolls-Royce.

50
Stagey

If actresses call themselves 'actors'
(A claim both bizarre and untrue)
By extension the men of the theatre
Must surely be 'actresses' too.

51
Business Class

Salesman Grundy,
Berne on a Monday,
Ostende Tuesday,
Meriden Wednesday,
Arles on Thursday,
Voss on Friday,
Dedu Saturday,
Beirut Sunday,
That was the week
Of Salesman Grundy.

52
Elusive

Solomon Grundy,
Bjorn on a Monday,
Kristin Tuesday,
Marit Wednesday,
Al on Thursday,
Wes on Friday,
Dai on Saturday,
Barrett Sunday,
Quite a conman
Suleman Gründig.

53
On Target

As Tracy starts to throw the darts
The venue's loud and full:
Just watch her check out one two nine –
Twenty-five... treble eighteen... bull.

54
Guided Missile

The Choirboy threw a well-aimed dart
When kneeling down to pray,
It pierced the wine-filled chalice
And the priest said, "Let us spray."

55
Games People Play

As he threw out the old carpet
Father said to son:
"Let's play civil servants –
You can be the tacks collecter."

As she cooked Sunday lunch
Mother said to son:
"Let's play railways –
You can be the plate-layer."

After playing in his bedroom
Son said to parents:
"Let's play waste management –
You can be the tip-tidiers."

56
Cockney Epitaph

Born,
Gorn.

57
Life in the Ark

Lions roared,
Bulls gored,
Wasps stung,
Limpets clung,
Hyenas shrieked,
Skunks reeked,
Frogs leapt,
Cats crept,
Snakes coiled,
Oxen toiled,
Fleas jumped,
Sloths slumped,
Horses neighed,
Donkeys brayed,
Monkeys teased,
Bears squeezed,
Pigs squealed,
Pythons peeled,
Pumas pounced,
Kangaroos bounced,
Vultures flapped,
Crocodiles snapped,
Dogs growled,
Wolves howled,
Cocks crowed,
Fireflies glowed,
Woodpeckers drummed,
Bees hummed,
Tigers clawed,

Beavers gnawed.

58
Camel

Shape lumpy,
Back humpy,
Legs clumpy,
Feet stumpy,
Ride bumpy,
Mood grumpy.

59
Burdensome

The dromedary's got the hump
That grumpy desert rover,
The camel's even grumpier
He's got the hump twice over.

60
Frog

Cold-blooded
So no sweater…

But a lovely jumper.

61
Snake

Be wary of the boa
When the sun is moving loa
And the village lanterns gloa
long the waterline.

Be wary of the boa
When the turning tide moves sloa
And your fishing boat you roa
long the waterline.

Be wary of the boa
From its top branch sliding loa
With its length uncoiling sloa
long the waterline.

62
Nightingale

By a copse on Luton's northern fringe
Where developers' roads
Reach out like tentacles for rural prey,
I got off my bike to listen:
A nightingale on a low bush
Sang its tripartite song –
The plaintive repeated note,
The liquid cadenza,
The staccato coda;
To left and right
Encroaching by the day,
The neo-Georgian closes
Consuming habitat like fast food,
Symbols of a new order,
Whose legacy will be silence
Where once was heard music.

63
Bird Talk

The swallows skimmed the surface,
The ducks went deeper,
The kestrels wavered,
The flamingos stood their ground,
The woodpeckers picked holes,
The ostriches took it in their stride,
The skylarks were up in the air,
The kiwis kept their feet on the ground,
The buzzards went round in circles,
The crows came straight to the point,
The robins called a spade a spade,
The albatrosses took the wider view,
The parrots expressed themselves colourfully,
The condors assumed the high ground,
The petrels were all at sea,
The owls were completely in the dark,
The wrynecks spoke obliquely,
The peacocks showed their true colours,
The thrushes opened a whole new can of worms,
The vultures had some bones to pick,
The pigeons couldn't see the wood for the trees,
The weaver birds tied up the loose ends.

64
Bird Etiquette

Don't snipe at mynah faults
Or avocet to then swan off.

Don't get raven mad
And skua tirade unfairly.

Be neither a shoveler at table
Nor a warbler in the bath.

Share a nightjar before loving
But no puffin in bed after.

65
On a Window Ledge

A pigeon descants
His suburban tone-poem
A high-coo haiku.

66
Cat

Alluringly distant,
Seductively cool,
Disarmingly playful
But nobody's fool.

Endearingly wilful,
Aloof from the crowd,
Bewitchingly haughty
And famously proud.

This lovable tyrant,
Beguiles and unnerves,
And makes of his master
A minion who serves.

67
Best Friends

Poodles
Have oodles
Of charm
To disarm.

While brave GSDs
Will track and seize
The fugitive crook
And bring him to book.

The Labrador's fun
Is to work with the gun
Retrieving game
His claim to fame.

While the sporty Jack Russell
Without any fuss'll
Dispatch the rats
And shame the cats.

The rottweiler's muscle
Equips him to tussle
Aloof and hard
The ideal guard.

While the border collie
Can herd without folly
No brain works faster
Than his, for his master.

And what an achiever!
The golden retriever
Such coolness of mind

When guiding the blind.

68
The Dog Trainer's Consolation

I've show dogs who hate being looked at,
And Yorkies who won't wear a bow,
I've gun dogs afraid of loud noises,
And huskeys who won't work in snow.

I've greyhounds who like running slowly,
And lap dogs who've learnt how to bite,
I've guide dogs who take the wrong turnings,
And guard dogs who won't work at night.

I've obedience dogs who are naughty,
Police dogs who won't grip a sleeve,
St Bernard's who won't work on mountains,
Retrievers who never retrieve.

I've companion dogs snubbing their owners,
And bloodhounds with no sense of smell,
But my own dog – a sweet rescue mongrel –
Is perfect, and that's just as well.

69
Designer Pets

A cog or a dat would suit me fine
With vices absent as virtues combine:
The feline hygiene, the canine devotion,
Someone else gets the crap and the lack of emotion.

70
Home Sweet Home

Said the doe:
"Home is where the hart is."
Said the bat:
"Home is where I hang my head."
Said the orang-utan:
"Home is up the wooden trunk to Budfordshire."
Said the sloth:
"Home is where I put my feet up."
Said the queen-bee:
"Home is where my honey is."

71
Rich or Poor

A guileless curate cycles in the rain,
His life is simple, self-denying, plain,
For cakes and ale don't rule out bread and wine,
To crave is human, to forgo, divine.

The rain falls also on a sullen youth,
(His appetites are all he knows of truth)
To duties blind, insistent on his rights,
The hand that feeds him is the hand he bites.

These two are equal in financial worth,
But one sees life's abundance, one its dearth,
For values make us rich or poor –
Such poverty's not cured by having more.

72
Shallow

In the fashion
In the swim
Your take on truth
A surface skim.

73
New Man

Original but uncontroversial,
Creative but confined,
Passionate but restrained,
Humorous but benign,
Masculine but emollient,
Admirable but contemptible.

74
Apologia

No. Freeing Barabbas wasn't my choice –
I acquiesced in the popular voice:
The common man's suspicious of wise saws,
Easier with base theft than lofty cause.

They condemned a man I felt worth sparing,
An innocent with a line in caring,
(But note my dexterity with the mob:
Yes. A clean pair of hands helps in this job.)

75
Elementary

Everything King Midas touched
Would turn at once to gold,
And when he touched his daughter
She too fell still and cold.

He'd lost the girl he treasured,
The child he longed to hold,
Whose life was far more precious
Than palaces of gold.

The alchemist had no such power –
The opposite, in fact –
The magic touch King Midas had,
Demonstrably he lacked...

For every mix and treatment
In crucible and mould,
Belied his wayward theories
And would not turn to gold.

But energy and hope remained
His failure's ghost to lay,
As self-belief and cheerfulness
Drove doubt and gloom away.

Two seekers for this element
And only one made gold,
Which caused the worst disaster
A father could behold.

Yet strangely for the alchemist
A better tale is told –
Of happiness – though what he touched

Would never turn to gold.

76
Comedienne

After the first joke
She waits for the laughter,
Her smile the rictus of terror,
Her eyes the unloved child's
Frantic for kindness.

77
The Obligation

Whatever happened to carol singers,
Songsheets crisp as snow,
Cheeks pink as apples,
Mouths round as spoons?

A new breed now calls,
Voice rough as glacier,
Tongue sharp as icicle,
Smile thin as starlight.

For a minute's ragged unison
I offer my jingle of coins,
Paying off what I owe
To those who used to call.

78
Family Values

My mother screws the 'Social',
My father traffics crack,
My sister offers massage,
My brother deals in smack.

My grandma works the 'plastic',
My granddad is a fence,
My cousin Beth's an escort,
My cousin Darren rents.

My uncle's in protection,
My auntie lifts up West,
While I nick cars to order
And ring them for the rest.

Our faith's the fig we couldn't give,
Our creed's the tinker's cuss,
There is no you or him or her,
There's us and us and us.

79
God's Estate

Our tower block's a temple,
Our flat a private shrine,
The urine in the stair-wells
The sacramental wine.

The pushers on the walkways –
Evangelists of crack –
Have promised once we're converts
There'll be no going back.

The burglars – theologians –
Exhort us seek true worth,
To lay up treasure elsewhere
But not on sinful earth.

The muggers on the landings
Remind the lax ingrates
Their ministry is threatened
By lean collection plates.

80
Parkbenchers

We are the closed accounts,
The guests you don't announce,
The worked-out mines,
The discontinued lines.

We are the seized-up locks,
The stopped clocks,
The crumbling beams,
The frazzled seams.

We are the lives merely token,
The griefs unspoken,
The unheeded curses,
The unfollowed hearses.

81
The Bystander

I am part of the pollster's sample
But never the single voice,
The also-ran at the interview
But never the final choice.

The reflex, never the stimulus,
The shadow, but not the soul,
The splinter, the shard, or the fragment,
The fraction, but not the whole.

The actor playing a minor part
Who's not in the press reviews,
The unknown face you see in the crowd
When somebody else makes news.

I'm a pencilled note in the margin,
But never the text itself,
The mortice, the tenon or dovetail,
But never the actual shelf.

The padding to fill out a story,
The flesh, but not the bone,
The adjunct, addendum, appendage,
The setting, but not the stone.

One vibrant voice in the cheering crowd
At somebody else's game,
One pair of hands in the world's applause
For somebody else's fame.